SANTILLANA · ALTAMIRA

ENRIQUE CAMPUZANO · JOSÉ A. LASHERAS

EVEREST

Text on Santillana: Enrique Campuzano Ruiz

Text on Altamira Cave: José A. Lasheras (Director of Altamira Museum and Research Centre)

Photographs: Manuel Blanco
        José A. Lasheras (pages 44, 45, 47, 48, 49, 52, 53a, 53b, 55, 58)
        Archivo Everest (pages 46, 50-51, 56-57, 59, 61, 64)

Editorial coordination: Francisco Bargiela

Layout: Gerardo Rodera

Cover design: Alfredo Anievas

© EDITORIAL EVEREST, S.A.
Carretera León-La Coruña, km 5 - LEÓN
ISBN: 84-241-3518-0
Legal deposit: LE. 638-1997
Printed in Spain

EDITORIAL EVERGRÁFICAS, S.L.
Carretera León-La Coruña, km 5
LEON (Spain)

· · · SANTILLANA · · ·

At daybreak the pale early morning light casts shades of ochre and yellow over the sandstone dwellings and shrouds the streets in evocative hues of grey.

Soon the sun rises up over the red roofs, silhouetting the overhanging eaves against the background of the blue sky. Climbing the walls are the running geraniums or *gitanillas*, the tropical Spanish moss, the ivies and the bougainvillea, imbuing façades and balconies with a blaze of colour.

On rainy days or after a storm has passed, Santillana's stones ooze moisture and one is struck by the smell of the earth emanating from the cornfields and that of livestock coming from the sheds and stables that still survive.

The peaceful afternoons drift sleepily by and are spent at home, once the demands of daily life have been appeased. All is peace and quiet, broken only by the babbling of brooks and the sound of horses' hooves. Occasionally a faint rumbling of engines is to be heard coming from local garages, the price we have to pay for modernity.

At nightfall darkness invades the streets of Santillana, barely lit by the traditional village lamps, and the visitor senses the peace his heart has yearned for, whilst the silence of the carved stones transports him faraway to times long past, times he knows so little of but which

Windows in the village of Santillana.

———————— ॐ ————————

have always been in his dreams.

Santillana perdures. Centuries have slipped by and generations of inhabitants have come and gone, but the wonders of Santillana have survived unscathed, a true embodiment of art, enchantment and fantasy, the rewards of which are reaped by the visitor in whose senses a lost memory is evoked, one which is brought back to life at every turn in what is a recreation of history.

Time has passed, but not without leaving an indelible mark. Santillana constitutes a vital landmark as we strive day by day to delve further into our cultural heritage, this being a land of natural toil, blood and sweat, lords and vassals, exploitation and famine, fear and betrayal, religion and rents, possessions and estates, aims and enterprises, colonial riches, stones and jewels, pleasure and art.

A SAINT AND A FLAT PLACE WITH NO SEA

Santillana is commonly known as "the town of the three lies", in reference to the meaning of its full name, *Santillana del Mar*, the accusation being that it is neither a holy place (*santa*), nor is it flat (*llana*) nor does it lie by the sea (*mar*). Nevertheless, as is the case with all such maxims, this one also contains a series of half truths.

Following pages: view of the village featuring the Collegiate Church.

Autumn balcony scene with flowers and ivy.

Door at the residence of Leonor de la Vega.

Truth to be told, the town does in fact owe its name to St Juliana (*Sancta Iuliana = Santa Yllana*), but this does not imply any holiness on the part of the place itself or its inhabitants. Santillana is indeed not a flat town, since, lying as it does in a hollow, its relief is one marked by gentle hills. Nor can it be said to lie on the coast, although its municipal district does reach out to the sea, at the village of Ubianco, at a league's distance from Santillana itself. The sobriquet "del Mar" (of the sea) would seem to serve to distinguish this town from that of Santillana de Campos, itself situated in the neighbouring province of Palencia, both towns having once been ruled over by the House of La Vega.

The truth of the matter is that about 1,200 years ago a group of monks came to settle in these parts, part of the few possessions they brought with them being an insignificant box of relics belonging to the aforesaid saint who, born in Nicomedia in Bithynia (nowadays

Turkey), had been martyred in the times of Diocletian, in the late 2nd century.

The foundation of the small monastery located in the area then known as Planes in all probability took place in the 8th century, although the earliest documentary proof of its existence dates from 870. The document in question is the first of those that make up the *Cartulary* or compilation of abbey records which, mostly of an administrative nature, trace the history of monastic influence in these lands, covering the periods of its creation and consolidation, its process of expansion, its subsequent crisis and eventual dissolution.

The monastery evolved around a small chapel that held the remains of St Juliana and which had become a place of worship and a pilgrimage centre. In time it would receive donations of lands, estates and small churches or monasteries, as a result of which both the prestige and patrimony it held in the region soared. Such development is to be seen within the context of the process of repopulation and colonization which, instigated by King Alfonso I of Asturias, swept the region from west to east and was based on the so-called *presura* or privilege by means of which the king granted the right of ownership to anyone who took charge of lands for farming purposes, to build houses or to found monasteries.

By this time a number of other places of worship had sprung up in the region, all of which would gradually fall under the influence of the abbey. Access to the latter was provided by a road network of Roman origin, which facilitated its relations with the surrounding area. It was not long before the small hamlet that had taken shape around the monastery achieved a certain degree of fame, so much so that its name would be changed from Planes to that of the patron saint of the monastery, *Santa Yllana*.

The subsequent history of the small monastery - which possibly pertained to the Benedictine order - was

Tagle family residence coat of arms.

one marked by steady, secure development until the year 1045, when Ferdinand I, king of Castile, granted it a series of privileges and exemptions, such as the right to collect certain taxes and not to pay others and the ban prohibiting the entry of *merinos* (royal governors) and judges. Such favours are indicative of the degree of respect that was already shown towards the monastery and the figure of the abbot.

THE PILGRIMS' ROUTE TO SANTIAGO

Once the Islamic invasion had been brought to a halt and the Moslem raids were held back beyond the Cantabrian Mountain Range, the relatively good connections enjoyed by this area and the fact that it lay directly in line with the capital of the Kingdom of Asturias, Oviedo, where King Alfonso II had erected a magnificent basilica dedicated to the Lord Saviour, *El Salvador*, led Santillana to become one of the most appealing staging posts for pilgrims who came this way as they headed for Oviedo and ultimately Santiago de

Calle del Río, with the Collegiate Church in the background.

Scene captured in Santillana.

Scene captured in Calle del Racial.

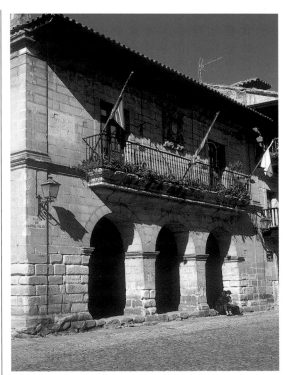

Santillana Town Hall.

Compostela, subsequent to the discovery of the tomb of St James in around 812.

In fact two of the oldest pilgrimage routes included Santillana on their itinerary. The first of these was the coastal route which, starting out from France and the Basque Country, passed through this area skirting the coast, taking advantage of large sections of the old Roman road that once linked the northern sea ports. Record is held of this route in the abbey cartulary in the form of a document dated 1107, by means of which the monastery was entrusted with the church and the jetty and boats at the nearby village of Cortiguera, the purpose of the latter being to help pilgrims cross the Suances ria or tidal inlet.

Another record dating from around the same point in time refers to the second such itinerary, the sea route to Santiago, which is described by the geographer from Ceuta, Al Idrisi, who mentions Santillana as being a religious centre worthy of

stopping off to see on the journey back by sea from Santiago to Bayonne.

Some indication as to the welcome that was afforded pilgrims throughout the Middle Ages and up to the time of the French Revolution is given by the two pilgrim hospitals that once existed in Santillana, one being under the patronage of the Velarde family and the other belonging to the Collegiate Church.

THE ABBOT AND HIS VASSALS

As early as 1043, Kind Ferdinand I had granted Abbot Juan and *Santa Juliana* several revenues and estates in the lands of Burgos, thus recognising the extensive jurisdiction awarded the monastery.

Simultaneous to the extension of monastic influence over most of the western half of this region from the 10th to the 12th century, all power in the area was seen to be vested in the figure of the abbot, whose

Above, and opposite, two views of the Collegiate Church of Santillana.

jurisdictional authority, acknowledged in a royal document dated 1045, was later to be further consolidated by means of the *fuero* or privilege that was granted Santillana by Alfonso VIII in 1209 and the appointment of the abbot as the lord of the town.

As was the case with most villages and towns in this region, the vassals of Santillana were allowed a free choice of lord (Santillana was a *behetría de mar a mar*, that is, a town whose inhabitants could select a lord with no restrictions whatsoever regarding the lineage of the latter). All three seignorial regimes - those involving rule by the abbot, the Crown and ancestral families - were represented here, although the predominant authority was that of the abbacy. The latter would nevertheless gradually wane in face of the rising force of the secular families, in particular the House of La Vega.

THE COLLEGIATE CHURCH

In all likelihood the conversion of the monastery into a collegiate church took place in the mid-12th century. Although it is not known for sure which monastic rule governed the monastery during the late Middle Ages, most evidence would seem to point to the Benedictine Order. However, as from the 12th century and coinciding with the construction of the new building, the Order of the Canons of St Augustine took charge of the monastery, where they would remain until the mid-19th century.

The original building on this site was a small hermitage, whose style was not far removed from that of the Visigothic or Asturian tradition and over which, in the course of the 12th century, the church we see today

was erected in Romanesque style, the latter having since undergone several alterations.

The church has an east end comprising three semicircular apses - the central one of which is the largest and tallest - covered by barrel and quadrispherical vaulting. It also features a crossing that boasts an outstanding elevation and a central lantern, the semispherical dome of which once rested on pendentives (converted into squinches in the 18th

Baptismal font. Relief depicting Daniel amidst the lions.

Detail of the Collegiate Church façade.

century). The body of the church consists of a nave and two aisles, the former being both taller and wider than the latter. Covering these vessels are a series of Proto-Gothic ogival or pointed vaults, some of which are dome-shaped whilst others feature ridge-ribs. They are the result of the alterations carried out on the building in 1256 owing to the state of complete ruin that the tower - which was rebuilt - and some of the church buildings had fallen into.

The various architectural elements of the church are clearly influenced by the International Romanesque. Thus, whilst its pillars clearly mirror those at Jaca Cathedral (Huesca), its spaces resemble those to be seen at Frómista (Palencia), the said edifices being two of the main centres responsible for the creation of this style.

Access to the interior is gained through a semi-circular-arched portal complete with archivolts that opens out from the southern wall onto a spacious atrium which, having originally been a cemetery, is guarded by a pair of stone lions crafted by a local artist in the 16th century.

Relief depicting St Anne and the Blessed Virgin at the Collegiate Church.

Running across the portal façade is a frieze containing small sculptures of saints arranged around an image of Christ Enthroned, itself enclosed in a vesica or *mandorla* borne by angels. The striking features of the frieze are its unsophisticated carving and the deterioration of the stone as a result of the passing of time. The niche crowning the tympanum (itself a 17th-century addition, together with the arched loggia to be made out above it) contains an image of St Juliana bearing the palm leaf symbolizing martyrdom and fettered to the devil of her temptations.

Rising up to the right of the portal is a cylindrical tower or belfry, reminiscent of the ones at Frómista. Adjacent to this lies the new sacristy built in 1699, and at the west end of the church stands the bell-tower that was reconstructed in the 13th century. The arcaded building that closes off the atrium on one side is the former chapterhouse, which features a Romanesque-style doorway and a Herrerian-flavour Baroque structure.

As soon as we step inside the church, we become aware of the lack of light and the sensation of heaviness provided by the thick walls. Likewise, we are struck by the semicircular arches and the Romanesque capitals, the iconography of which represents the struggle between Good and Evil using a series of allegories and symbols, such as fighting warriors or knights, real or fantastic animals and birds, true-to-life or geometrical plant forms and scenes taken from the Bible or popular legend, such as the creation of Adam and Eve or the episode when St George defends a maiden against the Dragon. Both of the latter are located in the Gospel aisle. Scenes of a more profane nature - either obscene or simply referring to the construction process - are to be found in the Epistle aisle.

Rising up at the centre of the crossing is the **Cenotafio de Santa Juliana**, a monument whose rather unrefined and simple memorial stone was placed here in 1453, when the Bishop of Burgos, Alonso de Cartagena, transferred the saint's relics - which had lain at this spot - to the chest that is worshipped today at the main retable.

The Gothic-style **main retable** was fashioned in the late 15th and early 16th centuries at a studio in Burgos

that displayed a Hispano-Flemish tendency and which was greatly influenced by the circle of León Picardo. The studio's patron, Diego Hurtado de Mendoza, Duke of the Princedom, is represented on the retable in a kneeling posture. The illustrated panels gracing the retable show scenes from the Gospel (Christ's Birth, the Epiphany, His Entrance into Jerusalem and Burial) and others depicting the life of the saint, as told in the *Leyenda Dorada* (Golden Legend) by Jacobo de la Vorágine. The lower panel on the Gospel-side section of the retable alludes to the martyrdom of Juliana: a soldier casts molten lead over her head as she hangs by her hair from a beam. In the scene on the opposite side, the saint, accompanied by the Devil, is presented before her husband, the judge Eulogio, who himself had tortured her for not having wanted to renounce her virginity and her faith in Christ; ultimately, she is decapitated. In the central section of the *corpus* of the retable, above the relic chest bearing the coat of arms of the House of La Vega, there appears a sculpted image of the patron saint. Still further up we see a portrayal of the Blessed Virgin with the Angels and an excellent Calvary crafted in a highly expressionist style. Adorning the vertical sections separating the retable corpus from its wings are images of the twelve apostles. Each is portrayed with his respective attributes: the book wrapped in a bag, and the symbol of his martyrdom.

The sculpted scenes gracing the predella are clearly to be attributed to another artist, one who was primarily influenced by the Renaissance style. They portray the four evangelists, complete with their respective attributes, in some cases showing them in natural postures, such as sharpening a quill or blowing on ink. On either side of the predella stand the statues of Sts Justa and Rufina.

The altar frontal is embedded with four Romanesque-style reliefs depicting Apostles which, together with the reliefs to be found in the side apses (images of the Blessed Virgin Mary with the Child and St Juliana with the Devil) and the statue of Christ Enthroned located in the baptistery, in all likelihood were part of a former monumental portal which, to be dated at around the

year 1200, either never actually materialized or has since disappeared. Stylistically speaking, this work is to be associated with both the artistic ensemble of Aguilar de Campóo and Carrión de los Condes and the representation of the Apostles in the Holy Chamber at Oviedo Cathedral.

In the 16th century a new chapel was added to the northern section of the transept. Dedicated to St Jerome, the chapel houses a mid-18th century Baroque retable featuring an excellent polychrome wood sculpture of Christ that has been attributed to Francisco Rincón, the master under whom Gregorio Fernández, the greatest exponent of Castilian Baroque art, learnt his trade.

Above left, detail of the retable.
Below left, St Juliana and the reliquary chest. Retable,
Collegiate Church.
Below right, image of Christ in the Chapel of St Jerome.

Collegiate Church of Santillana. 12th-century Romanesque statue of Christ Enthroned.

The opposite arm of the transept contains the **sacristy**, the work of Gregorio de la Roca (1699), with a marble lavatory and a very fine drawered piece of furniture (*cajonería*). Its highlights are several 13th and 14th-century Gothic images, a late 17th-century Hispano-Philippine ivory statue of Christ and a number of Baroque reliquaries. The sacristy also houses a collection of early 16th-century silver jewellery, such as the processional cross crafted by the Burgos artist Pobes, the reliquary of St Juliana, a chest adorned with filigree and two Gothic maces, along with several Baroque chalices and two large Mexican trays which, bearing the mark of San Luis de Potosí, were donated in 1687, together with the magnificent high altar frontal, by Luis Sánchez de Tagle, an *Indiano* or Spaniard who had made his fortune in America.

Lying next to the sacristy doorway is a Romanesque sarcophagus, allegedly that belonging to Doña Fronilde, a great benefactress of the monastery.

In the early 18th century, the stone choir was built at the west end of the church, featuring a wrought iron grille, stalls fashioned in walnut and an outstanding, beautifully designed and recently restored **organ**.

Beneath the tower we find the **baptistery**, boasting as it does a large Romanesque font bearing a relief that allegorizes the life of grace, above which is displayed the excellent Romanesque representation of Christ Enthroned that formerly graced the main portal that is no longer in existence.

THE CLOISTER

Square in shape, the cloister opens out into the Gospel aisle through a Romanesque portal. Once the church structure had been completed, the cloister was added to the latter in the late 12th century. Noticeably the ensemble lacks all the remaining habitual monastic buildings, such as the refectory, the kitchen, the dormitory and the stores. The chapterhouse is situated adjacent to the atrium. Such an arrangement is owed to the fact that the new order of canons were not obliged to live in a cloistered community and thus could take up residence outside the religious enclosure and as a result had no need for any of the said buildings.

The most important feature of the cloister is the iconography to be seen on its capitals, which bring together the main decorative, figurative, geometrical and vegetable motifs marking the historical and thematic evolution of the Romanesque.

The southern section adjoining the church is the oldest part of the cloister and its capitals reflect a wide range of images taken from the Bible, such as Christ Enthroned and the Tetramorph, the Apostles, Daniel in the Lion Pit, the Dream of Nebuchadrezzar, Samson Slaying the Lion, the Beheading of St John, the Miracle of the Bread and the Fish and the Descent from the Cross. These are accompanied by a series of other themes of a more profane nature such as the Knight's Farewell or those illustrating the struggle between Good and Evil, examples of which are the scene of the dragon-slaying Christian warrior (a copy of an Assyrian relief dating from the 6th century B.C.) and the depiction of the wolf-fleeing shepherd. Worthy of special attention is the capital portraying a knight fighting a great dragon. Being similar to that crafted by Pedro Quintana at the nearby church at Yermo (1203), this capital has given rise to the supposition that the cloister at Santillana is the work of the same artist and was created around the same time as the one at Yermo.

The capital carvings lining the western passageway of the cloister comprise both allegorical representations of Purgatory, featuring fantastic intertwining creatures (following the tradition of the cloister capitals at Silos), and other purely geometrical adornments (in keeping with the Norman or Arab traditions). The highlight of this section is the capital depicting Heaven and Hell, in which St Michael is seen weighing souls - here represented by little heads - and spearing the devil, who himself attempts to tip the scales in his favour.

The remainder of the capitals decorating this arcade and the northern passageway feature motifs from the plant kingdom. Dating back to as early as the 13th

Opposite, detail of the Collegiate Church cloister.

Two-page spread overleaf, the cloister and the following capitals adorning the same:
1.- The Last Judgement.
2.- Intertwined griffins.
3.- Warrior slaying the dragon.
4.- Daniel amongst the lions.
5.- Crucifixion.
6.- The knight's farewell.

4

5

6

Southern arcaded passageway of the Santillana Collegiate Church cloister.

century, they reveal a clear Cistercian influence (and are derived from those at Aguilar and San Andrés del Arroyo).

Erected in the 16th century, the eastern arcaded passage is divided into a series of funerary chapels pertaining to the noble families of Santillana, as is the one located at the southwestern corner of the cloister, itself bearing the coats of arms of the Polanco family.

All around the arcaded passageways lie a series of Romanesque and Gothic tombs which, recovered from the cloister court, belong to abbots, canons and nobles, the identity of the latter being deducible from the coats of arms and inscriptions they bear. Also to be seen here are a number of Romanesque corbels that belonged to the eaves of the church roof at the time of the alterations undertaken on the façade in the 17th century.

The Collegiate Church of Santillana, together with its cloister, was declared a Monument of National Interest in 1889.

CAPITAL OF LAS ASTURIAS DE SANTILLANA

Although the 12th and the early 13th centuries were to prove to be the time of greatest economic development and jurisdictional expansion in the history of the monastery, they would also mark the beginning of its gradual decline. This period witnessed the conversion of the local economy from that characterized by the direct exploitation of lands, salt mines, rivers, windmills and livestock to one which, based on ground rent, brought immediate cash profits to abbots and canons alike.

*Plaza de Ramón Pelayo as seen from the colonnade beneath the Don Borja Tower. Two-page spread overleaf,
Casa del Águila and Casa de la Parra.*

Torre del Merino.

The year 1250 marked the beginning of a time of increasing internal tension and mounting external pressure, at the root of which lay the rise of the secular nobility. The latter, eager to possess their own income and lands, constituted a serious threat to the collegiate chapter, which in order to defend its interests had to resort to the provisions of the *fuero* or town charter and the royal privileges it had been granted.

During the 15th century, the pressure exerted by the nobility continued, aided by the crisis in which the Castilian monarchy was engulfed. The process whereby all power in the region was transferred to secular hands reached its peak when King John II of Castile conceded rule over the town to the Marquis of Santillana.

This new stage in the town's history, in which Santillana became the capital of an extensive region encompassing most of the western half of present-day Cantabria - referred to as the *Merindad de las Asturias de Santillana* (in contrast to the other *Asturias*, of which the capital was Oviedo) -, saw the shaping of a new centre of civil authority in what was then the *Plaza del Mercado* or Market Square (today called *Plaza de Ramón Pelayo* in honour of the Marquis of Valdecilla, a great benefactor both of the town and the region who had returned to Spain after making his fortune in America). Around this square, at which a weekly market had been held ever since the granting of the town *fuero* or charter, a series of towers and fortified houses were erected, such as the *Torre del Merino* (the Governor's Tower, that belonging to the king's representative in the town) and the *Torre de Don Borja*, the property of the Barreda family, both of which are Gothic in style and date from the 14th and 15th centuries, respectively.

*Don Borja Tower
and the Domingo Barreda residence.*

Velarde Palace.

Another view of Velarde Palace.

Thus the urban layout of Santillana began to take on its characteristic form - that of a letter "Y" -, one that with only very slight alterations has remained unchanged from the 15th century to the present day and whose development has revolved around the two hubs of religious and administrative authority, namely the Collegiate Church and the Square, and has been determined by a strict set of regulations that forbade any construction to be undertaken without due authorization (Council Ordinances of 1575).

What was permitted, however, was the redesigning and the erection of new buildings on sites that already existed. The said Ordinances also record the local trades, quoting those of blacksmith, tailor, carpenter, butcher, master mason, official, shoemaker, day labourer and domestic servant. On sale at the weekly market held in the Square were the typical products of the region, such as bread, cheese, fish, lard and fruit, together with handicraft items from Galicia, Burgos and Bilbao, which could also be purchased in the local shops.

Once the old village of Santillana had stretched out beyond the shadow of the monastery, owing to the new dwellings erected to accommodate canons and vassals, plans were drawn up for a street called *Rúa del Rey* (King's Road). Records of the existence of this street date back as far as the 13th century. Lined by a series of houses, plots of land, orchards and framyards, *Rúa del Rey* ran from the Collegiate atrium itself to *Calle Santo Domingo*, where it merged with *Calle de Juan Infante*, which in turn led out into the Market Square. The cobbled streets are known to have existed at least as early as the 17th century.

In the mid-15th century, the population of Santillana was 800, whereas in the 17th and 18th centuries, the period in which the town's economy truly flourished, it reached around 1,000, a figure that has varied only slightly up to the present day, the current total being 1,300. At that time, the municipal area was divided into four districts or cantons, and the four fountains to be seen in the town today were already in existence, bearing the names of: La Vieja, El Cantón, La Fontanilla and El Revolgo.

Apart from the *Casa de la Villa* or Town Hall, the other public buildings in Santillana were the prison, located next to the present town hall, and a school which, funded by the town at least from the late 17th century on, had one teacher for grammar and another to teach children to write. Higher education studies in Theology, Grammar and Arts were conducted at the "Regina Coeli" Convent. The Town Council also provided a doctor, a surgeon or blood extractor, a barber and a chemist. In the area know as Campo del Revolgo, an oakwood at the exit to the town on the way to Puente San Miguel, the representatives of the valleys met (the council members themselves convened in the Collegiate atrium) and received the royal envoys. There was both an inn and a post office here. This was also the venue for livestock fairs and the pilgrimages held in honour of St Juliana and St Roque (whose chapel lies opposite the Diocesan Museum) and the popular local fiestas, festivities in which fun and recreation were guaranteed. It is known that in the 17th century bull races were held, along with jousting tournaments, dances, bonfires and games involving canes, skittles and cards.

Above, residence of Leonor de la Vega; below, the "Gil Blas de Santillana" parador.

NOBLE LINEAGES, MANSIONS AND COATS OF ARMS

In 1445 King John II conferred the town of Santillana to Don Iñigo López de Mendoza, the renowned Castilian poet, who thus became the first Marquis of Santillana in what was a further strengthening of secular seignorial dominance. Some years later, in 1512, the abbot would eventually renounce his claim to the lordship of the town.

Nevertheless, the unwillingness of the people of the region to be subjected to any ruler other than the king gave rise to a prolonged dispute (the so-called *Pleito de los Valles*), which lasted almost two centuries and would never be resolved in their favour, since Santillana itself and its surrounding districts were to belong to the jurisdiction of the Duke of El Infantado (the successor of the Marquises of Santillana) right up to the 19th century, when the *Ayuntamiento* or Town Council was formed.

The honour of serving as representatives to the king or the marquis was shared out amongst the members of the families of most noble descent - those of Barreda, Bustamente, Villa, Velarde and Polanco -, who were thus able to enjoy noble status and fashion coats of arms displaying impressive carved mottoes alluding to honour, pride, triumph or fame. The motto of the Villa family reads "A good death brings honour upon a whole life", whereas that of the Cos family says: "Lay down your life for honour and your honour for your soul". Others invent traditions linking the family with legendary heroes, such as that shared by the Velarde and Tagle families: "Velarde (or Tagle) was his name, he who the serpent did slay (a reference to St George) and the Infanta did marry". Although most of the inhabitants of the area were in fact *hidalgos* or noblemen, this did not imply that there were no great economic differences existing between them, nor that in the Baroque era scores of so-called hidalgos were living in nothing short of abject poverty.

Dating back as they do to the Gothic, the symbols used on the coats of arms mostly refer to trades, place names or legends, although some, such as the sirens, plumes and leaves, are a reflection of the exoticism and abundance to be found in America.

In the Baroque period, the typical residences belonging to the local nobility - both in the town itself and in the surrounding region - were the so-called *casonas* or

Above, the Villa family residence, nicknamed that of "the well-built men".
Opposite, detailed shot of the coat of arms on the façade.

stately mansions. To quote the words of Ortega y Gasset, "the truly great aspect (of houses such as these) is not so much their size as their pretensions... Indeed, these buildings have such an imposing presence and are seemingly so self-absorbed and presumptuous, that we tend to look on them as being palaces..." The difference between a *casona* and a palace is basically one of size (palaces are normally larger, free-standing buildings) and of the descent of their respective owners. Along with the Gothic towers, the Renaissance palaces and the Baroque convents and monasteries, these stately homes constitute the most representative architecture of the region.

Rising up in the former Market Square (today *Plaza de Ramón Pelayo*) is the **Torre del Merino** or Governor's Tower, which possibly dates from the 14th century.

The Quevedo y Cossio family residence.

The Tagle family residence.

Owing its name to the fact that it served as the residence for the king's representative, the tower to a large extent retains its original appearance, with only a few alterations (such as the battlements converted into windows under the roof and the ground floor flat-arched window). The interior of the tower is graced by a beautiful wooden structure.

Torre de Don Borja was built in the 15th century, its fabric being added to in the 16th. The tower was named after Don Francisco de Borja Barreda, who in the 19th century became the last member of his family to hold possession of their entailed estate. Comprising two sections joined by an inner courtyard, the tower structure underwent restoration in 1981 in order to house the Santillana Foundation, which at present uses the building as a cultural venue where a number of important exhibitions have been held.

Standing as it does in *Calle de la Carrera*, **Torre de Velarde** was erected by García Velarde in the mid

15th century. It has a square-shaped ground plan and is vertically divided into three levels, the outstanding features of which being the pointed-arch doorways and the foiled and ogee-arched windows. Adjacent to the tower once stood the first hospital that took care of pilgrims making their way to Santiago de Compostela.

Casa de Leonor de la Vega. Although traditionally connected with the mother of the first Marquis of Santillana, this residence would seem to have been built at a somewhat later date, around the late 15th and early 16th centuries. Set between the flat-arched windows of the upper storey are three Gothic coats of arms belonging to the House of La Vega. Worthy of admiration are the iron fittings on the doors that give access to the residence. The façade at the back of the

*Outside view and hallway of Peredo Palace
(also called Benemejís Palace).*

building features several Renaissance elements and opens out through an arcade onto a beautiful orchard.

Palacio de Velarde. This palace is situated in *Plaza de las Arenas*, adjacent to the Collegiate Church. Commissioned by Alonso de Velarde, it was built in the mid 16th century in a Renaissance style, a fact borne witness to by the main façade which, lying to the east, includes arcading, balconies and coats of arms. The façade that gives onto the square itself displays a feature characteristic of this kind of palace, namely a staggered gable end adorned by pinnacles. Perhaps the most outstanding element of the building is the parapet belonging to the main quarters, framed as it is by Plateresque ornamentation and the Velarde coat of arms.

Casa de la Parra and Casa del Águila. The first of these former residences owes its name to the great vine (Sp.: *parra*) that adorned the façade until it was replaced by the wooden framework we see today. Dating from the early 16th century, the building was designed in keeping with the Gothic tradition, as is to be observed in the entrance doorways and the side façade, the latter featuring paired pointed-arch windows.

The 17th century saw the adding on to this building of the *Casa del Águila*, so-called due to the eagle (Sp.: *águila*) carved on the Estrada y Tagle coat of arms constituting the focal point of the façade. Other noteworthy features of the façade are its arcading, parapets and projecting balcony, all of which are typical of the noble Baroque architecture of this region.

Parador "Gil Blas". This state-run hotel was built in the late 17th century by a member of the Bracho lineage, a family that later was to become related to the Barredas. From the outside it has a more sober appearance than the other palatial residences in Santillana. A spacious hallway leads through to a vestibule or foyer, around which the various service quarters are located and from where a staircase rises to the main floor. The building became part of the National Parador Network in 1944.

Casona de los Villa. Standing at the entrance to Santillana in *Calle Santo Domingo* is the Villa residence. This structure features a Gothic section that was extended in the 18th century, as is witnessed by its flat-arched entrance doorway, its bull's eye windows and pulpit-shaped balconies.

Casona de los Hombrones. Having also belonged to the Villa family, the name of this building (Sp.: *hombrones*, well-built men) refers to the spectacular coat of arms and in particular the supporters bearing its shield and the motto that reads: "UN BUEN MORIR ES ONRA DE LA VIDA" (A GOOD DEATH BRINGS HONOUR TO LIFE). Its construction possibly dates from the late 17th century, as is evidenced by its arcade and projecting balconies.

The **Ayuntamiento** or Town Hall ranks as one of the most elegant buildings in Santillana. It manages to bring together the palatial character of its urban setting with the noble architecture representative of the rural environment. Although its origins are to be traced back to the 18th century, as from 1835 the building underwent far-reaching alterations in order that it might serve as the seat of the Town Council. Dating from this period is the coat of arms on its side façade, featuring the town shield and crested by the coronet of the Marquisate of Santillana.

Casa de los Quevedo y Cossío. Lying adjacent to the local watering hole, this building comprises two square-shaped dwellings. The Quevedo residence - the family armorial bearings being displayed over its parapet - features excellent masonry and a vaulted passageway for the stream into which the said watering and washing place drains. In addition to its fine flat-arched doorway, on its continuous projecting balcony the Cossío residence boasts one of the most remarkable coats of arms in all Santillana.

Casona de los Sánchez de Tagle. Situated in the area of Santillana known as El Campo del Revolgo, this residence was built in the late 17th century by Don Andrés, brother of Don Luis (the first marquis of Altamira), Don Anselmo, bishop of Michoacán (Me-

Exterior of Regina Coeli Convent.

xico) and Don Pedro (who had been in charge of the *Consulado* or mercantile court in Mexico), all of whom had made their fortunes in America. An original feature of the building is its continuous balcony on the upper storey, above the magnificent family coat of arms. Inside is an excellent archive and art collection which lend the house a seignorial atmosphere in keeping with its past glory.

Palacio de Peredo. Standing at the entrance to the town, this palace was also built by a noble with an American connection, Don Francisco Miguel de Peredo, who from 1694 served as Knight of the Order of Calatrava. Erected as it was over the site of a previous residence, the building preserves in its grounds remains of the former Gothic structure. It is without doubt the most elegant palatial edifice in the whole town. The severity and geometrical nature of its Classicist façade contrast sharply with the sheer exuberance of the coat of arms which, adorning the latter, is supported by lions and is replete with mantles, sirens, masks and plumes symbolizing the exoticism and opulence of America. Surrounding the building is a splendid park of great botanical interest owing to the rare species it holds. Other outstanding features of the palace are its extraordinary library and its art collection.

Palacio de Bustamente. To be found in *Calle de la Carrera*, this palace is very similar to the one we have just described, although it is somewhat smaller and more austere. It was built in the mid 18th century by Don Francisco Antonio Bustamente, whose coat of arms featuring thirteen roundels and bordered in French style by cannons, pikes, pennants and drums stands out over the door of the central balcony, protected by great eaves. Remarkable features are its solid, well-squared masonry and the side pulpit-shaped balconies.

Casa de los Abades. This residence is located adjacent to the atrium of the Collegiate Church and was

House of the Archduchess.

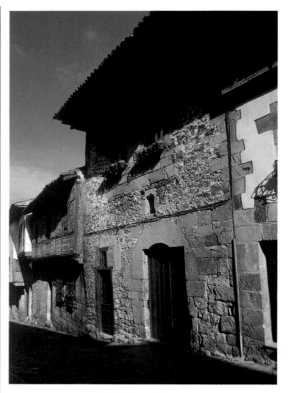

Jesús Otero Tower.

once also known as the *House of Archduchess Margaret of Austria*, having served as the residence of the latter when she fled her homeland on the fall of the Austro-Hungarian Empire. It was built in the late 17th century and a century later came to belong to the Barreda Bracho family. The coats of arms are modern, the work of Jesús Otero, and include the emblems belonging to the most notable of the town's noble families.

The coat of arms of the founder of the **Palacio de Valdivieso** looks down from the corner where *Calle del Cantón* and *Calle de las Lindas* converge. The building itself is an example of the 18th-century urban palace featuring a flat ashlar façade with numerous timidly enhanced windows and slightly projecting balconies. Today the palace is a hotel. The very same fate has befallen the **"Los Infantes" building** in Avenida Le Dorat (so-called after the French town twinned with

Santillana), which itself has a superb façade that was brought here from the neighbouring village of Oreña three decades ago.

On the outskirts of Santillana, on the road leading to the village of Camplengo through La Fontanilla, we come across the so-called **Palacio de Chamberga**, an 17th-century edifice that in its staggered side gable ends - fashioned in the style of those of the Palacio de Arenas - reflects both the endurance and the origin of Renaissance structures.

Baroque religious architecture is represented in Santillana by two important monasteries that were erected at the entrance to the town.

The Dominican monastery of Regina Coeli (**Convento de Regina Coeli**) was established in 1592 by Don Alonso de Velarde, lord of the palace situated in *Plaza las Arenas*. Upon the death of the latter, however,

Alonso's son Pedro wished to have nothing to do with his father's foundation. Later, in 1692, the Duke of El Infantado took over the patronage of the monastery and it was under his auspices that the present-day building was erected, and its church being consecrated shortly followed by the cloister.

Subsequent to the process of ecclesiastical disentailment or *desamortización* introduced by Mendizábal (1837), the monastery was abandoned and later taken over by a community of nuns belonging to the Order of St Clare who still run the convent today. At present, the building houses the Diocesan Museum and its offices.

The **convent of San Ildefonso** was founded in 1667 by the canon-treasurer of the Collegiate Church, Don Alonso Gómez de Corro, whose house survives adjacent to the church apses.

Young noblewomen belonging to the major local families and the great regional lineages would enter the convent to become Dominican nuns. Architecturally speaking, the convent is similar to the monastery described above, although its cloister is more secluded. Inside the convent church there is a magnificent image of Christ which, sculpted from Philippine ivory in the late 17th century, presides the high altar.

THE DISCOVERY OF SANTILLANA

Santillana's current role as a town of major cultural importance tends to overshadow the various economic alternatives that have prevailed throughout the town's history.

Subsequent to a first, somewhat prolonged stage of agriculture-based subsistence economy that lasted until the 19th century, the town's modern economic existence has been one based on livestock farming or a combination of the latter with industrial activity in the region of Torrelavega. Recently the focus of Santillana's economy has shifted towards the services sector in light of the increase in tourism, which today constitutes the town's main source of income, one which has arisen as a result of its cultural attractions.

National recognition of Santillana as a unique artistic ensemble is to be traced back to the 18th century, when it made its first appearance in world literature by means of a picaresque novel by the French author Alain René Lesage, who in his *Histoire de Gil Blas de Santillane*

A typical street in Santillana: Calle del Cantón.

(1715) locates the main character here. In the late 18th century, Jovellanos included in his *Viajes* ("Travels", 1798) a superficial description of the town revolving around its Collegiate Church. At a later date, certain Romantic travellers (such as the English author Borrow) were to consider Santillana to be an evocation of times gone by. However, fellow Cantabrian José María de Pereda showed little appreciation for the town, there being not a single reference to it in any of his novels. The true champion of the cultural wealth of Santillana would be Amós de Escalante, the writer responsible for arousing interest in local artistic treasures, in particular those gracing the Collegiate Church cloister, which in *Costas y Montañas* ("Coasts and Mountains") he referred to as "a precious little jewel of Romanesque art".

Benito Pérez Galdós (author of *Cuarenta Leguas por Cantabria*, "Forty Leagues around Cantabria", 1876) is held to be both the literary discoverer of Santillana, the town which as he put it evokes feelings of "solitude and silence", and the great promoter of its cultural appeal, one that is still felt today. To quote his own words, "Nobody shall be able to say: 'I saw Santillana on passing through'. In order to truly see the town, one simply has to visit it."

A number of other artists helped to spread word of the town's beauty, such as Málaga-born Ricardo León, who set his *Casta de Hidalgos* ("Caste of Noblemen") here, along with authors of the calibre of philosopher Jean-Paul Sartre, Emilia Pardo Bazán, Unamuno, Ortega

Two exhibits on display at the "Regina Coeli" Diocesan Museum. Left, the Bielva monstrance. Above, the Castro Urdiales image of "Ecce Homo", the work of Gregorio Fernández's studio (17th century).

y Gasset, Concha Espina, Gerardo Diego, Jesús Cancio and José Hierro.

However, it was to be the discovery of the Altamira Cave in 1879 - and the subsequent debate amongst experts as to the exact age that should be attributed to it - that would give rise to enormous expectation in and around Santillana which upon the confirmation of the authenticity and chronology of the cave paintings would trigger off great cultural interest in the town. To a large extent this interest emanated from members of the Catalonian and Madrid aristocracy that were related to the noble families of Santillana or to the Marquis of Comillas and who proceeded to purchase the town's towers and palaces and to sponsor a series of artistic and

literary evenings. Amongst the most prominent of these figures were Count Güell, the Marquis and Marquise of Benemejís and the priest of the Collegiate Church and historian, Don Mateo Escagedo Salmón.

After the Spanish Civil War (1936-39), the official institutions promoted what can be called an elitist form of cultural development, the materialization of which was a series of temporary exhibitions and meetings of intellectuals. The most renowned of the latter was the so-called *Escuela de Altamira* (Altamira School, 1949-50), a forum for aesthetic meditation which opened up the way for contemporary art and gave Lafuente Ferrari the opportunity to write his magnificent work entitled *Libro de Santillana* ("Book of Santillana").

PRESENT-DAY SANTILLANA

The historical evolution of Santillana and the fact that its physical appearance has been preserved throughout the centuries has conditioned the predominantly cultural role played by the town in the present day. Santillana - with the aid of the Altamira paintings - has become an internationally renowned centre of attraction, one which is actively involved in that new way of life and new form of understanding leisure that is known as "cultural tourism".

Jesús Otero Museum.

Thirty years ago the first cultural institutions in the town designed to transform Santillana into such a centre for culture were born.

Firstly, there was the restored cloister of the "Regina Coeli" Convent, which was converted into an exhibition hall. The most outstanding of the displays staged here was the Group Abstract Art Exhibition which, based on the work of the *El Paso* group, provided the inspiration for the Cuenca Museum.

In 1967 the **Diocesan Museum** was established in the Regina Coeli Convent, the aim being to recover, study, exhibit and conserve the religious art heritage of the Diocese of Santander. At that time the diocese was in danger of disappearing as a result of the passing of time and the new liturgical standards issued by the Vatican II. The latter recommended greater austerity in church decoration and thus led to retables and images being withdrawn from worship and often abandoned. In all probability, these religious works of art were either stolen or disposed of.

On display in the spacious rooms, corridors and cloisters are works from most of the villages of the region. The museum thus allows us to admire the peculiarities of religious art, in particular that dealing with popular religiousness, along with works belonging to the great artists of the Baroque Castilian and Andalusian creative centres (Gregorio Fernández or Martínez Montañes) and those of America.

Today about a thousand works of different techniques and styles are shown, ranging from the Romanesque to that of the present day. The highlights of the museum are the extraordinary collection of polychrome-wood popular religious images, the collections of Spanish and colonial silverware, and those of enamelled objects, Philippine ivories, Chinese silks and an impressive collection of images of Christ, donated to the museum by Father Cué.

Two-page spread overleaf: the "Regina Coeli" Diocesan Museum.

The Goat's Fountain.

The Museum boasts a highly prestigious Restoration Workshop that satisfies private demand, a technical team committed to providing advice for parishes, and an educational section whose task is to conduct students' visits. The same building also houses the Documentary Diocesan Archive, of vital importance to anyone wishing to get to know the history of this region, an institution that also maintains its own workshop devoted to the preservation and restoration of books. Consequently, the museum is to be regarded as a highly significant cultural centre, one which collaborates with both public and private entities.

The Santillana Foundation (*Fundación Santillana*), established in 1981, has earned a reputation as an institution of great prestige. Its premises occupy the Tower of Don Borja and the former residence of Infanta Paz, the sister of King Alfonso XII, the reconstruction of which was awarded a prize by the *Europa Nostra* Association.

The aim of the foundation is to project universal literature and art on an international level whilst emphasising Hispano-American and Cantabrian culture. It achieves this end by holding a series of momentous exhibitions, courses and symposia, as well as by producing its own publications. Although such activity takes place all year round, it is in summer when it reaches its peak and stages greater quality events.

The range of cultural activities on offer in Santillana has been increased by the emergence of further cultural centres over the last few years. Perhaps the most significant of the latter is the **Regional Ethnographical Museum** (*Museo de Etnografía Regional*), located in the *Casa del Águila* and *Casa de la Parra*. Nowadays the building belongs to the Cantabrian Regional Department of Culture, which uses it as a venue for temporary exhibitions in the fields of art and Cantabrian ethnography.

Last but not least we have the **Jesús Otero Museum** (*Museo Jesús Otero*), situated adjacent to the Collegiate Church atrium. On display within the museum building and grounds - the renovation of which was carried out by the Municipal Restoration School and Workshop - are a series of works that this great Santillana-born sculptor (1908-94) donated to his home town. Other works by Otero can be seen at various points around the town, such as the "Monument to Altamira Man" standing at Plaza Ramón Pelayo and the so-called Goat's Fountain or *Fuente de la Cabra* in the Campo del Revolgo area.

Finally, no account of Santillana should overlook the recent tendency to convert the town's palaces and mansions into venues for artistic or cultural exhibitions. Two notable examples of this are *Casa de Sánchez de Tagle* and *Palacio de Pereda*. This myriad of activities and attractions do full justice to the cultural reputation and image that Santillana has earned both on a national level (in 1943 it was declared a Site of National Historical and Artistic Interest) and on an international plane, having been nominated to be included as one of the monumental sites belonging to UNESCO's *Heritage of Mankind*.

·· ALTAMIRA ··

ALTAMIRA

Constituting as it does a world-famed monument, Altamira Cave is perhaps the most popular of the Spanish contributions to the Heritage of Mankind, the cultural inventory created by UNESCO. Such universal repute has led the cave to earn its place in the select ensemble of artistic manifestations that, wherever one may be in the world, inevitably serve to identify Spain. The great popularity of Altamira and the representative function it performs are to be put down to the truly unique nature of many of its features, as a result of which the cave simply cannot be restricted to the narrow context of any particular cultural region.

In order to ensure the conservation of the cave, the amount of people that are allowed inside each year is limited to eight thousand five hundred. Prior to the introduction of these current restrictive measures, however, Altamira was one of the most frequently visited monumental sites in Spain, alongside the Prado Museum and one or other historical enclave lying within the areas of Spain that attract mass tourism.

Marcelino Sanz de Sautuola, the discoverer and first researcher of the Altamira Cave.

— ꕔ —

All this is of course unmistakably linked to the image of the famous polychrome bisons that grace Altamira. Indeed, so impressive is this particular ensemble of cave art that it has come to completely overshadow both its own archaeological and pre-historic context and the rest of the artistic manifestations dotted around the cave. Let us now take a closer look at what are the most spectacular paintings belonging to prehistoric man. The aim of the short account that follows is to afford the reader a comprehensive introduction, both in artistic and historical terms, to Altamira, the very first milestone in the history of world art.

SITE LOCATION, DESCRIPTION AND SETTING

Located on *Monte Vispieres*, Altamira Cave is to be found at the top of one of the gently-rising calcareous elevations flanking the small valley in which the town of Santillana lies. The only entrance to the cave faces north and stands at 156 metres above the present sea level. Lying five kilometres from the sea, it is a little over two

Solutrean-type points or arrowheads, carved from flint.

a

kilometres away from the nearby River Saja. Stretching out over a total length of 270 metres, the cave features a main passage whose height varies from 2 to 12 metres and whose width ranges from 6 to 20 metres. Its ceiling is very near to the land surface, the average distance separating it from the latter along the entire length of the cave being approximately 11 metres.

The cave floor is made up of a series of parallel and practically horizontal strata of limestone rocks (calcarenites) which, featuring thicknesses of between 0.3 and 1 metre, are separated by very fine clay layers. A remote period of karstic activity occurring as far back as the Pliocene was to give rise to the openings which, as a result of a series of subsequent deeper collapses and fractures, would gradually endow the underground area with its present shape, one characterized by trapezoidal sections and flat roofs.

Visitors to Altamira today are afforded a beautiful view from its strategically placed *mirador* or vantage

point. Looking out to the south, we are greeted by the Cantabrian Mountain Range and, rising up even further in the distance, the *Picos de Europa* mountains, which for long periods of the year appear capped in snow. Whichever way one looks, the surrounding landscape is one of hay meadows sown to provide fodder for the cattle kept on simple family-run farms. The vestiges of formerly extensive woodland still remain, as do scattered clusters of trees and other trees that are used together with shrubs to form hedgerows and reinforce the low stone walls marking off small adjacent lands. The scenery unfolding before us is a vast, irregular green mosaic created by man with the aid of a wet, mild climate in the area encircling the monumental town of Santillana.

**AN ACCIDENTAL FIND
AND A CONTROVERSIAL DISCOVERY**

About 14,000 years ago, a group of people of varying ages - boys and girls, men and women - abandoned what we know today as Altamira Cave. Exactly why they left or where they were headed for is not known, but there is no record of any other people ever having occupied the cave subsequent to their departure. Behind them they left a number of broken, worn out or simply forgotten tools, innumerable remains of their food (mainly animal bones and marine mollusc shells) and, the product of their hearths, large quantities of ash and charcoal scattered all over the spacious "vestibule" area next to the mouth of the cave. Likewise remaining were the paintings and engravings that were to be found all around the cave and which are of such great interest to us... We simply do not know, however, whether these people intended ever to see or use their paintings again, or whether they aimed to reoccupy this site at a later date.

Shortly afterwards, a great natural collapse or rockfall occurred at the cave, as a consequence of which the entrance to the latter was completely blocked. Over five metres of the rocky overhang under which numerous human groups had lived during the Upper Palaeolithic suddenly came crashing down. Thereupon the rainwater that ran down the hillside, dripping into the cave, gradually formed a stalagmitic crust over the fallen stones and earth, thus completely closing the cave, sealing it off from external conditions and shrouding the remains that had been left by the people who once lived there.

In the mid 19th century this very site was covered in bushes and undergrowth. At that time, and with the aid of gunpowder, good-quality stone was extracted from the immediate vicinity for construction purposes in the neighbouring districts and villages. Today one can still make out the shot holes and other marks left by this activity on the rocky outcrops. Consequently a sound theory has been put forward maintaining that such quarrying work and the explosions it entailed may well have led to the cracking of the solid layer sealing the cave. Thus, around the year 1871, a farm labourer named Modesto Cuvillas from a nearby village was to become, as he himself put it: "the single true discoverer of Altamira Cave... and the person who showed the cave to several people, one of whom was Don Marcelino Sautuola... regardless of whether the cave is of any historical merit, I am the first man to have seen it in the present age...". These words have been taken from a document written by Cuvillas in which he claimed some form of economic reward for his part in the discovery of the by then famous Altamira.

Solutrean and Magdalenian arrowheads, made from flint and antler, respectively.

Ⓐ

Two kilometres away, at Puente San Miguel, lay the residence belonging to Marcelino Sanz de Sautuola, a well-educated man (a Law graduate from Madrid university) who besides possessed a fair fortune. As a scholar he displayed above all a profound and all-encompassing scientific curiosity, both in the field of History and that of Natural Science. He was an antiques enthusiast and kept collections of minerals, fossils and insects.

Indeed, it can be assumed that Sautuola's first visit to Altamira in 1876 came about as a result of his avid interest in geology. He managed to explore the whole cave, his great motivation spurring him on to overcome the many difficulties involved in such an undertaking. In the deepest-lying of the cave's chambers, he came across some strange black drawings to which he at first

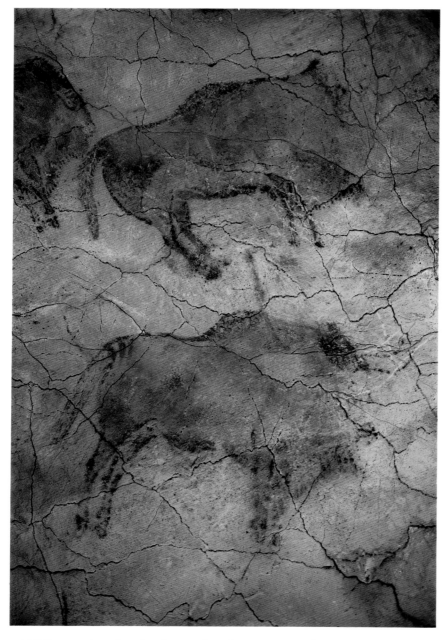

paid little attention, deeming them to be of no great importance.

As Sautuola himself has told us, "Goaded on by my enthusiasm for such studies and excited above all by the numerous and extremely interesting collections of prehistoric objects that I was fortunate enough to see on several occasions at the Universal Exhibition held in Paris in 1878, I determined to conduct some research in this my own province...". A decision which was to bring him back again to Altamira.

In 1879 he performed a series of excavations in the part of the cave nearest the entrance. Lying amongst other remains, he found several tools crafted from stone and bone. It would seem that one day when he was involved in this excavation work, his daughter María accompanied him to the cave, and she was to be the first to notice the figures painted on the ceiling, crying out to her father: *"¡Papá, bueyes!"* ('Daddy, oxen!'). Sautuola was dumbfounded by this find, as nothing of this kind had been known of before. However, he now fully realised the potential implications and the great significance that his discovery might entail, and became even more aware of the obstacles that he was going to en-

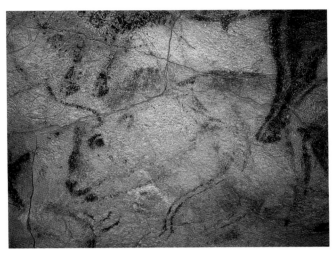

A black bison's head at the centre of the Ceiling of the Polychromes.

counter in order to obtain unanimous recognition and acceptance of the cave's authenticity.

A year later in 1880 he published a well-documented booklet entitled *Breves apuntes sobre algunos objetos prehistóricos de la provincia de Santander* ("Brief Notes on Certain Prehistoric Objects in the Province of Santander"). The booklet opens with an account of the finds he had made at a cave in the district of Camargo and then goes on to deal with Altamira. In reference to the latter, he provides a description of the remains corresponding to human occupation, namely stone and bone instruments, adornments, mineral pigments and traces of food such as shells and bones... Sautuola was careful to furnish all kinds of complementary information, such as the fact that no pottery was to be found and that all the remains were covered in a limestone layer. Later on in the booklet, he describes and analyzes the cave paintings, identifying them as representing the extinct bison and applauding the great artistic merit he believed the set of paintings and their creators deserved. Finally, he relates the paintings with other objects of prehistoric art crafted from bone, antler or ivory that had been found in France. He also established relations between the items found and those belonging to other European sites and between the mineral pigments of the soil and those used in the paintings. He concluded his account of Altamira by accurately dating both the human occupation remains excavated and all the paintings observed as belonging to the Palaeolithic.

This find, that involving the oldest and most surprising of the arts created by mankind - rather than the cave stumbled upon by a hunter or the drawing noticed by an innocent child! - constitutes the *real* discovery of Altamira. A discovery which, not to be put down to pure chance but rather to the methodically planned work of a highly educated man, was to open up new horizons in our knowledge of prehistory.

Naturally such an important find as this was not going to be readily accepted even by the most open-minded of scientific communities. In the eyes of the scientific establishment, everything seemed to be excessive: the quality of the figures, their sheer magnitude and their age. Few were those who accepted the paintings, and thus recognition of what was the first art of mankind - due to the ignorance, excessive prudence and mistrust shown by the scientists - was delayed. Indeed the discovery at Altamira was to all effects officially overlooked and ignored, until in 1901 further caves also featuring fine paintings were found in France.

In 1902, E. Cartailhac, who to a certain extent belonged to the scientific vanguard of the day, felt obliged to rectify the stance he had taken and published

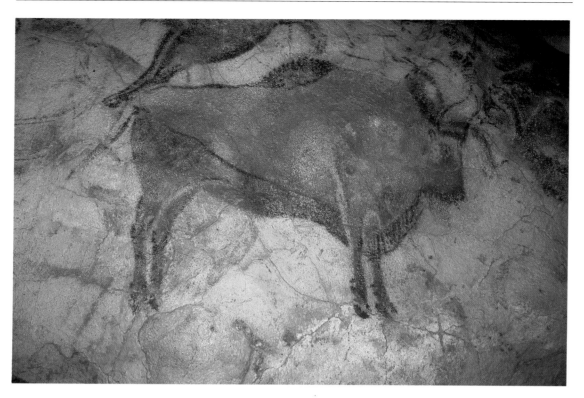

A standing bison, one of the most representative paintings of the "Ceiling of the Polychromes".

———————— ℭ ————————

an article - not bereft of certain humble tones - entitled *Les cavernes ornées de dessins, La Grotte d'Altamira (Espagne). Mea culpa d'un sceptique*, in which he acknowledged the fact that he had been: "...a party to an error that was made twenty years ago, an injustice that now has to be admitted and publicly atoned for. ...One must simply face the facts, and I personally feel obliged to do justice to Mr. Sautuola".

That same year Cartailhac visited Altamira for the first time, accompanied by H. Breuil. They were preparing the first major publication devoted to the cave. He also paid his respects to María, who as a girl had been the first person to see the polychrome figures. Her father, Marcelino Sanz de Sautuola, had died in 1888.

In 1908, J. Dechelette was to coin a name for our cave that would meet with unanimous approval, being the first to refer to it as "the Sistine Chapel of Quaternary Art".

THE ARCHAEOLOGICAL EXCAVATIONS AT ALTAMIRA

The first archaeological excavations carried out at Altamira were those undertaken by Sautuola in 1879. After meeting Cartailhac and Breuil, a pioneer figure in Cantabrian prehistoric studies, Hermilio Alcalde del Río, was to conduct a series of excavations in the cave as from 1902. His findings were published both in one of his own works and as an additional chapter to that of the two French prehistorians.

In 1924 and 1925, Hugo Obermaier, a highly prestigious German geologist and archaeologist who lived and worked in Spain for many years, undertook the most comprehensive excavations of those carried out to date, analyzing 40 square metres of the area between the mouth of the cave and the painted ceiling.

The most recent archaeological excavations were those performed in 1981 by Joaquín González Echegaray, who was at that time the director of the Altamira Museum.

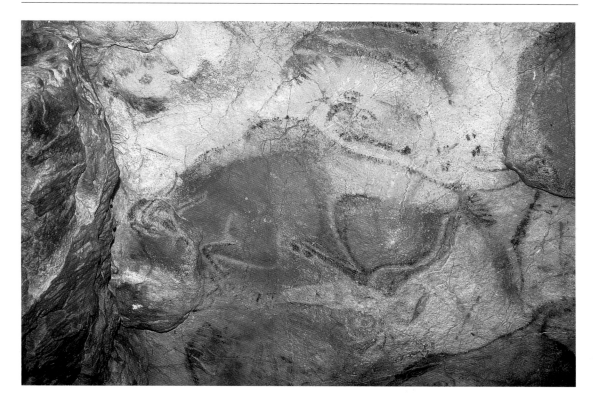

A curled-up bison with its head turned.

However, the oldest indications we possess of human presence at Altamira were not in fact the fruit of any of the above-mentioned excavations. A number of stone tools belonging to the Lower Palaeolithic were simply found lying on the ground by Obermaier himself. Other similar tools have likewise been discovered purely by chance on the ground at various points nearby. These finds are possibly to be related with the work undertaken to widen the road leading to the cave and the building of a car park near the entrance. An age of around 100,000 years has recently been suggested for all the tools, which basically consist of chopping tools, cleavers - bifacially worked artifacts commonly referred to as "stone axes" - and both end and side scrapers. The people who made these tools and used them to cut up their prey belonged to the genus *Homo* but are to be assigned to a different species from ours. Naturally their lifestyle bore absolutely no relation to that of the people who later inhabited the cave and adorned the walls with paintings.

The excavations have revealed the existence of two very rich archaeological levels. The lowest-lying and oldest of these belongs to the Solutrean culture and was formed as a result of the human occupation of the cave around 18,500 years ago. Amongst the stone tools found at this level are a wide variety of characteristic flintwork points featuring a concave base or a notch with a projecting lip on one side to make it even easier to affix the point to a wooden shaft. Each of the various types of points found appear in a range of sizes and calibres, the smallest of which can be associated with arrowheads and the use of bows. Burins, scrapers and the odd percussion tool for flaking purposes complete the list of the most important items of the stone collection. The bone industry includes awls (points for piercing holes), gravers and pendants.

As far as faunal remains are concerned, the bones that appear in the cave as a residue of the food consumed by its inhabitants tell us of the presence and relative abundance of deer, horses and bison, as well as the great interest shown by the people of that time in their capture. It would appear that goats and chamois were hunted to a lesser degree. Some lynx, wolf and fox bones are also present.

Lying just above the Solutrean level is the Magdalenian. This new period of human occupation of the cave has been dated as having occurred 15,500 and 14,000 years ago. On observing this level one is first of all struck by the lack of lithic industry and the practical disappearance of flint points that seem to have been replaced by those made from antler and bone. Working tools are well represented (needles, spatulas, instruments for smoothing leather, wedges, pierced antler rods or *bâtons de commandement*, etc.) and perhaps the most outstanding feature of this level is the abundance of harpoons and the sheer variety of their decoration.

One of the highlights of this level was the discovery of several deer scapulas on which engravings had been made, in most cases depicting hind heads. These figures feature the use of scratch and groove shading techniques in order to reproduce changes in the colour of the animal's skin at the front part of the neck and to generally fill in certain areas or to enhance a given anatomic aspect. Other deer scapulas displaying an identical theme and the same graphic technique were found on the Lower Magdalenian levels of the El Castillo Cave (in Puente Viesgo, 20 km from Altamira) and in other caves situated halfway along the Cantabrian coastline. This would seem to point to the existence of a regional cultural community, an interpretation that is also arrived at with regard to the geographical distribution of certain signs, industrial techniques and typological groupings.

However, the importance attributed to these engraved scapulas does not stop here. At Altamira and in other caves lying at the heart of Cantabria, we once again come across deer (along with other animals), this time engraved on the walls but using the same scratching and grooving technique. In all likelihood these engravings date from the same time as the

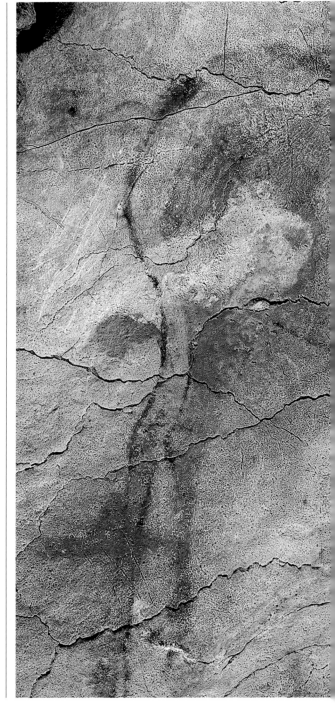

─────────────── a ───────────────

Magnificent image of a hind at one end of the ensemble of polychrome paintings.

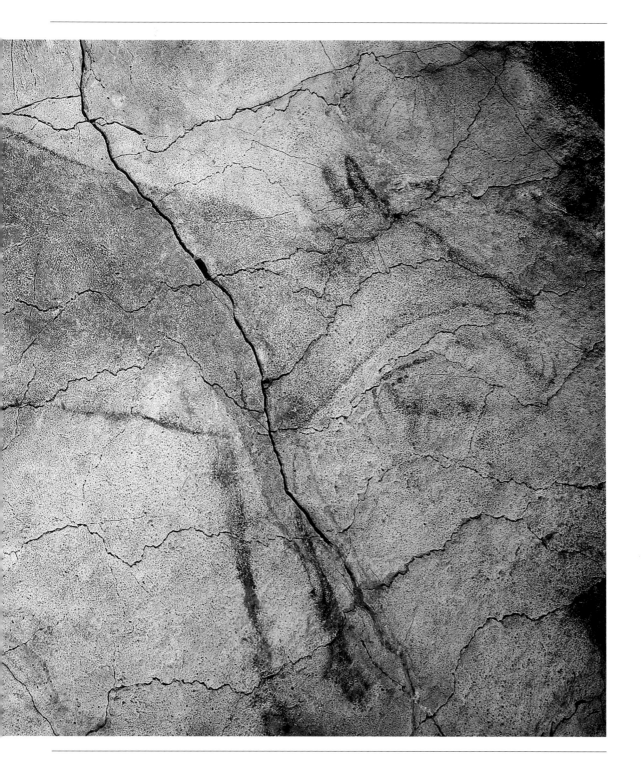

Above, a horse painted in red. Opposite, above: nail-shaped signs on the Ceiling of the Polychromes. Below, bison drawn in black only (charcoal), in the same style as the polychrome paintings and appearing amongst the latter.

scapulas. Furthermore, the fact that they appear in both a superimposed and underlying position with regard to other wall art manifestations would further support the idea that the dating of scapulas and engravings are indeed very close.

The fauna appearing on this level in the form of vestiges of hunting activity and the remains of food is virtually the same as that present on the Solutrean. What is noticeable is the increase in the percentage of deer remains and the reduction in that of the bison and the horse. There is also a rise in the number of fish remains and an abundance of limpet and winkle shells. What we see here, then, is a series of remarkable variations that on the one hand would appear to be due to changes in nature (climate, flora and fauna), but which to a greater extent are the result of cultural changes brought about by the human group in their relation with the environment. In short, complex and far-reaching changes, of which diet is merely a symptom.

THE PREHISTORIC LANDSCAPE

Up to the present point in time, no palaeobotanical studies have been carried out at Altamira. In order to give some idea as to the vegetation surrounding the people who lived here 15,000 years ago, we have to resort to information that is held on other caves. The fact is that in the said caves we find a large quantity of pollen from herbaceous plants but in contrast very little from trees. The predominant tree species thus identified are pines, birches, junipers and, to a lesser degree, oaks, alders and hazelnuts.

Generally speaking the climate in those times was cooler and wetter than it is today. The coldest periods, occurring during the Solutrean, were to feature average temperatures up to 10º lower than those of the present day, whereas temperatures during the Magdalenian occupation would be considerably milder. This would imply the existence at Altamira of a completely different

flora from that which we find today, one capable of sustaining a fauna similar to the one appearing today in other, more northerly regions of Eurasia and America.

The local fauna - identified by means of the food remains belonging to the human groups - points to a landscape necessarily featuring both expanses of meadowland (bison and horse) and areas of woodland (roe deer and wild boar). Even though the red deer, a less demanding or less environment-specific animal, can adapt to herbaceous landscapes, in light of its abundance here it would seem to be more logical to consider it as indicative of a mixed environment, that is, a "park"-type landscape in which the wooded areas - both deciduous and evergreen - would be limited in extension or where there would be formations of scattered trees, depending on the particular microclimatic features. The characteristic geographical nature of this region, featuring as it does impressive mountain ranges, the proximity of the sea and a fluvial network of small, short, parallel valleys gave rise in the Upper Palaeolithic to a highly varied environment well-suited to occupation by human groups. With the possible exception of the periods of extreme cold occurring 20,000 years ago, this area was never to experience the icy rigour of the central European arctic tundra or the French steppes. In the latter environments the art of Upper Palaeolithic caves often includes an abundance of animals such as the reindeer, the mammoth, the long-haired rhinoceros and even the musk ox, a fact which leaves no room for doubt regarding the temperatures and the landscape that prevailed in the last glaciation. In the Cantabrian region, on the other hand, the reindeer and the mammoth were scarce and are likewise equally scarcely represented in local cave art and food remains.

THE INHABITANTS OF ALTAMIRA

On the basis of the data provided by archaeological excavations with regard to both the natural environment and the material culture at Altamira, we can now venture a portrayal of the human groups who lived here 18,000 and 14,000 years ago. At the outset it should be borne in mind that this period is normally referred to as that when the technique of collective hunting flourished. Such an affirmation is supported on the one hand by the existence of outstanding, practically universal artistic manifestations - painting and sculpture -, and on the other by the degree of perfection and sophistication that had been attained in stone and bone working techniques, as is illustrated by the Solutrean flint points and the Magdalenian antler harpoons.

The provision of food for the inhabitants of Altamira simply has to have been based on hunting. The presence of remains belonging to both young and adult deer would suggest that the periods of occupation were long in duration, not seasonal, and that the hunting technique employed - that of stalking the prey - was not selective as regards which member of the herd was to be attacked. No evidence has been found anywhere to prove the use of traps, but in any case it would appear that they were not of vital importance. However, the use of hand-thrown weapons and rigid spear-throwing devices is evident, and although we cannot be totally sure about the use of bows, the only possible explanation regarding the purpose of some of the flint points found - which, owing to their minute size, presumably served as arrowheads - would seem to depend on our accepting the existence of this kind of weapon.

What does seem to be certain at Altamira is the great importance of deerhunting and the fact that this animal was increasingly preyed on by the humans. The most ubiquitous and seasonally stable of the species found here, the deer can be captured without serious risk to the hunter. Even though a horse or a bison may well provide a greater quantity of meat, this potential advantage diminishes when we bear in mind the greater seasonal mobility of these animals and the danger involved in hunting large bovids. Here we should remember that the only cave art scenes that have been interpreted as depicting accidents in which the hunter appears to have come off worst all feature bison, the most famous example of this being the painting at Lascaux.

The hunting of small mammals such as the hare is to be seen as being complementary to that of the deer, whereas the capture of other animals - for instance, the fox, the lynx and the wolf - was motivated by the use of their skins in the production of clothes.

Throughout the Upper Palaeolithic, along with the evolution of hunting techniques, a diversification of food resources is to be observed. Thus, molluscs and river and estuary fish such as trout and salmon become

increasingly important in the Altamira diet. As far as vegetables are concerned, these may have supplemented other foods and clearly had a strictly seasonal importance, but in any case no evidence supporting this has been reported.

A certain idea as to the clothing worn by the humans at Altamira is given by the slender bone needles featuring diameters of as little as 2 mm and holes through which thread made of gut or tendons could be passed. Needles such as this must have been used to sew together fine animal skins that had been previously worked and tanned. Moreover, the clothing thus produced is surely much closer to the attire created by Eskimos and other historical peoples of America than to the coarse image often assigned to these ancestors of ours.

Just as there were sites at which several species were hunted all year round, we also know of other enclaves whose hunting activity focussed almost exclusively on one particular species, whether this be the deer, the goat or the chamois, and which featured short seasonal summer-autumn occupations at the foot of the great

Cluster of black signs in the narrow end corridor (Section X). Two-page spread overleaf, close-up view of the group of bison.

mountains. In such cases a cyclical occupation of the territory would seem to prevail, featuring a series of programmed seasonal movements and small groups of humans scattered around the area at sites displaying certain specific characteristics. Other archaeological sites apparently reflect either a permanent occupation or a place of concentration or even both, another sign of the latter being elements of mobiliary or cave wall art which are seen to appear together only at the major sites or sanctuaries. Altamira is without doubt one such site.

ALTAMIRA CAVE ART

Art of course plays a vital role at Altamira, although as we shall see, it is also a source of frustration. Altamira cave art beautifully and evocatively opens up a door to

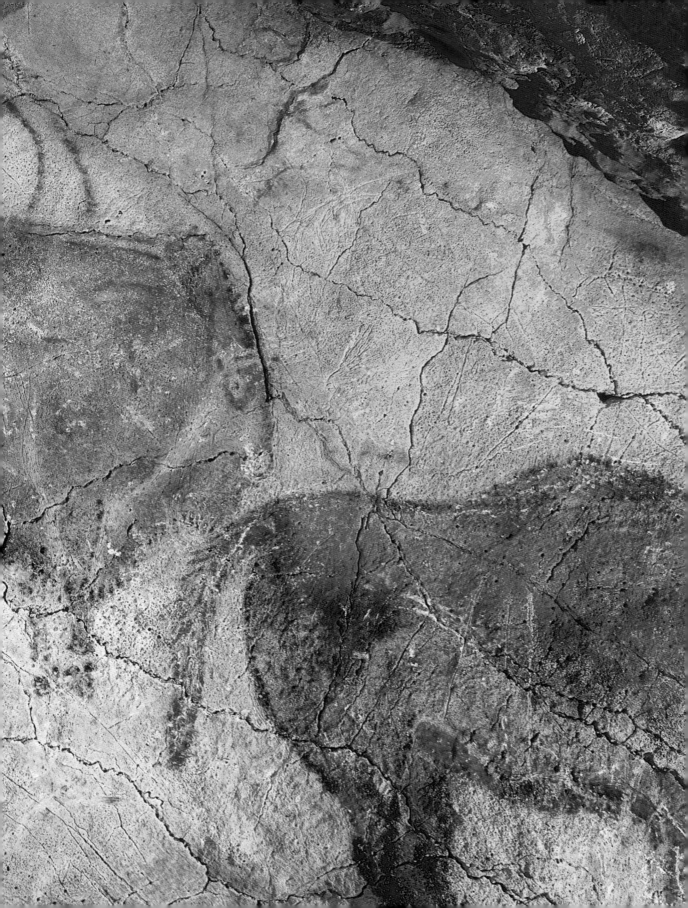

*Hind engraved using the characteristic technique of
shading the figure with grooves (Section III).*

the intellectual or spiritual world of those who created it.
Behind this door, however, there is more darkness than
light and we are afforded only incomplete views, pale
reflections of something that as a result we are unable to
fully comprehend.

Next to the living area of the cave and bathed in the
dim natural light from the mouth of the northward-
facing cave, we come across the renowned **Ceiling of
the Polychromes (Sp.: *techo de los polícromos*)**.
On analyzing the superimposed paintings and
engravings, we discover, at the part of the ceiling
farthest away from the entrance, a number of
monochrome red figures. Identifiable amongst the latter
are four outlined or monochrome-shaded horses, a goat,
and several hands, which likewise are drawn either as
outlines or as shaded figures. Here there is also a
number of more dubious figures such as what seems to
be an elk and a series of enigmatic signs and red stains

appearing in direct contact with other figures and
polychrome paintings that have clearly been
superimposed. It would appear, therefore, that the said
mysterious figures are the oldest creations to be seen in
this varied and colourful ensemble. Unfortunately, their
state of conservation is such that they are not easy to
make out, any appreciation being further hampered by
the fact that the figures lie low down close to the
ground.

In the rest of the cave, the use of red is repeated only
once, in a little chamber featuring a group of signs, the
most outstanding example of which measures two
metres in length. This chamber is indeed a most
extraordinary place, one which invites us to ponder the
true purpose of its paintings, since in order to appreciate
the said sign one has to practically lie down on the
ground; furthermore, it is virtually impossible for more
than two or three people to observe it at the same time.

The red Altamira paintings cannot be dated directly
owing to their exclusively mineral composition.
However, in light of their relative position on the Ceiling
of the Polychromes and the stylistic features they

display, it is possible to link their creation to the Solutrean occupations.

Easily distinguishable from the rest of the images is a series of figures drawn using a black charcoal outline. Although they are spread more or less all around the cave, these figures display a certain degree of homogeneity. Thus, on the Ceiling of the Polychromes we find several horses and one or two goats; in Section III we see a solitary bull and a frieze comprising two horses and two goats. In Section V there is a horse, whereas Section VI features three goats, a hind's head and a magnificent, simple bison. Lastly, in the narrow end corridor we come across two masks, a horse, a goat

Stampeding bison on the Ceiling of the Polychromes.

and a group of roof or hut-shaped signs. Dating has assigned these latter figures - and in principle the whole series - an age of 15,440 years, which coincides very closely with the dates obtained for the various Magdalenian occupations.

In order to observe the most recently created group of paintings, we have to return to the famous ceiling area. What we have before us here are none other than the magnificent polychrome figures dated as being between 13,940 and 14,710 years old. Without doubt these paintings constitute one of the masterpieces, not just of prehistoric art, but of art in general. Indeed, their sheer artistic quality was to be the reason why their discovery would arouse such great confusion and mistrust. Their discovery was simply something that had not been planned and for which no-one was ready. It all occurred too soon. The polychrome figures represent 21 bison, two horses and a hind in a variety of sizes ranging from 1.5 to 2.25 m. The following description tells us the manner in which they were created. First of all, by means of the techniques of engraving and charcoal, which were performed almost simultaneously, the outline and certain anatomical details of the animal - eyes, ears and horns - were drawn. A second stage involved the uniform, massive application of the reddish-hued shading colour, which was made by dissolving mineral pigments (such as ochres and hematites) in water. Subsequently, the mass of colour would be worked upon, certain areas being reduced by scraping and others left as they were in order to create separate planes and thus add relief to the animal anatomy in what can be virtually considered to be a *chiaroscuro* technique. The beauty and plasticity of the paintings are further enhanced by the artists' inspired use of the natural relief of the cave ceiling and the texture of stone. Moreover, the polychromatic sensation evoked in the eye of the observer is heightened by the colour of the underlying rock which is to be explained not so much by the way in which the paint was applied, but rather by the subtle erosion process it has undergone in the course of time. Also to be associated with these polychrome paintings are a series of bison drawn using black only and which, displaying a faded inner area, are almost identical to the former in form and style.

It is a far more difficult task to give a general overview of the numerous engravings that are dotted all around the cave. According to the style theory laid down by A. Leroi-Gourham, the frieze depicting horses is to be assigned to the initial period of this technique, featuring as it does a form of deep engraving that highlights only one profile (Section III). Another group of fine surface engravings portraying a series of goats and deer (Section V) likewise display certain archaic characteristics, and the same can be said of several bison which, appearing throughout the cave, have horns that are shown in a head-on perspective and bodies that are merely suggested by the lines outlining the animals' backs.

A large number of deer and the occasional goat engravings are to be found in the passage at the end of the cave called "The Horse's Tail" (Sp.:*Cola de caballo*, Section X), the deepest and hardest to reach of all the sections. In other parts of the cave, we see the association of deer and horses, but generally speaking the most numerous engravings found are those depicting deer and hind, and it is to the latter that the technique of groove-shading has been applied, thus making them that much easier to date.

Singular works that remain to be mentioned are the engraving of a bull (Section IV) and others portraying bison in false copulation and a horse. The latter, situated adjacent to the masks at the end of "The Horse's Tail", display a form and a symbolism similar to those of the group of polychrome paintings.

Once again it is on the Ceiling of the Polychromes that we are to find the greatest number and the best quality examples of this particular art form. Practically all the engravings on the ceiling underlie the large bichrome bison. Here we can see - albeit with difficulty, special lighting being required - a series of hind heads with groove-shading, identical to others found in the other sections of the cave. Amongst the remaining engravings gracing the ceiling there are some vaguely human forms that have consequently come to be known as "the anthropomorphs" and which are similar to those to be seen in other caves, as well as a number of other representations of horses, goats, etc. Standing before us on the right-hand side of the ceiling is the engraving of a mighty bellowing deer.

THE REASON UNDERLYING THIS EARLIEST ART FORM

A consideration that must be taken into account at this stage is that the emergence of art is linked to the presence of modern man, *Homo Sapiens Sapiens*, the human species to which the whole of present-day mankind belongs.

The value of all art, even most of the so-called decorative or applied arts, cannot be limited to that of mere ornamentation or adornment. Neither can anything that we refer to as art, whatever era it may belong to, be interpreted as simply the gesture of an individual, but

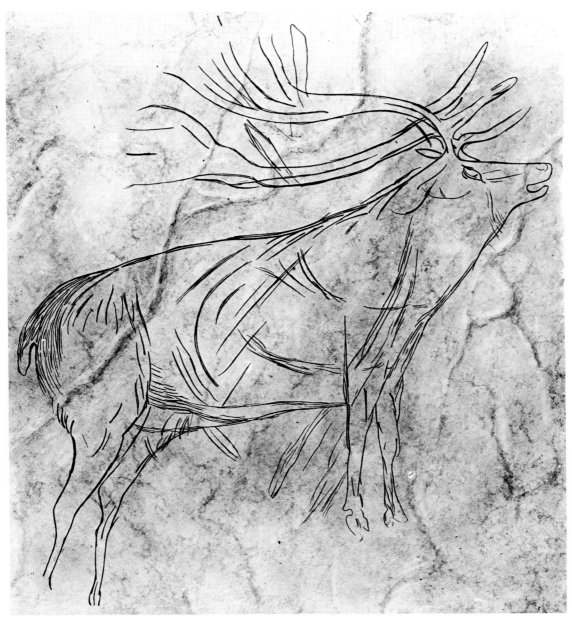

Engraving depicting a large bellowing deer.

rather has to be seen as a response to motivations and issues of key importance that affect all the members of the group in which it unfolds. This becomes even more apparent in the case of Palaeolithic cave art when we bear in mind that the latter was mostly performed outside the living areas, in dark, inaccessible places. It was soon to become clear to those who studied Prehistory that the paintings and engravings of Palaeolithic caves did not constitute an aesthetic leisure occupation or a form of entertainment. They were, without a shadow of a doubt, manifestations of high symbolic value.

Right from the beginnings of the study of this art, an attempt was made to explain the reasons underlying its existence, by means of ethnological comparison with contemporary societies of hunters/gatherers. Some believed that the images could constitute the representation of certain totemistic aspects, but the sheer diversity of the species portrayed in each cave, along with other considerations, invalidate such an interpretation.

Another school of thought tried to establish a link between the animal figures, and even the signs, and a hunting tradition involving the practice of sympathetic and propitiatory magic (whereby it is believed that the act of drawing the animal will help the hunter to kill it). However, it has been confirmed at many sites that the relative percentage assigned to each of the species hunted bears no relation whatsoever to the frequency of their appearance in paintings or engravings. Moreover, a series of other difficulties arise on attempting to evaluate not only the number of representations of a given animal, but also their relative importance as reflected by, amongst other factors, their size and their predominance within a group. As an illustration of these problems, we can quote the case of the Lascaux cave in France, where, although almost 90% of the fauna remains are attributed to the reindeer, the latter species is scarcely represented on the cave walls. At Ekain in Spain, the overwhelming majority of the images represent horses, whereas most of the bones found on the site belong to the red deer and the goat, horse bones in fact being practically inexistent. There is a long list of such examples. In any case, this kind of data is purely relative, since an animal's bones can neither reveal the amount of meat they once bore - their true nutritional value - nor inform us as to other superimposed intellectual and cultural values that may have been attached to any of the figures represented. Returning to the case in hand, how is the apparent importance of the polychrome bison at Altamira to be assessed in light of the dozens of red deer engraved all around the cave? There is no doubt that these images possess a certain added value, a symbolic content that surpasses that of the mere representation of an individual belonging to a given species.

Nowadays each cave is looked at from a global perspective, as if it were a sanctuary or one of our great old cathedrals, the conception of which is essentially of a unitary and synchronic nature, even though they house a series of time-honoured traditions and are subjected to frequent changes and additions that are integrated into the whole. Cave art comes within the sphere of what we understand as mythical or pre-philosophical thought, bordering on or lying within the realm of religion, the latter being interpreted as a vehicle for social and cultural integration. The caves are one of the places where this religious aspect is apparent, revealed as it is through certain discernible patterns in the use of the available space in each cave and by means of a visual language that has in part survived to this very day.

In specific reference to Altamira, and to the "polychrome paintings" in particular, it has been suggested that the bison figures represent a herd of adult male and female bison, a scene that would generally have occurred when the females were on heat. The differences observed are the typical ones that exist between individuals of the same species and have been captured by someone who in addition to being a hunter was also an artist. This interpretation based on the identification of a herd, together with a number of other considerations, allows the group of paintings to be associated with ideas and rituals concerning not only animal fecundity but also human fertility and survival. A further possible interpretation at Altamira, in keeping with the above, establishes a link with rituals performed to mark the reaching of maturity, rituals that are so important to humans today and which were even more so to contemporary prehistoric peoples.

Whilst for many years scholars have searched for the reason underlying the cave art of the Palaeolithic, at the present point in time the view is held that for such an extensive cultural manifestation as this - both in terms of time (stretching out over 20,000 years) and space (encompassing Portugal, Spain, France and Italy) - there simply cannot be a single common cause or just one interpretation. Today, therefore, we are witnessing a time of profound reevaluation and detailed analysis of the phenomenon of cave art, a process that has to include Altamira and which must be carried out before other syntheses can be put forward.

··· INDEX ···

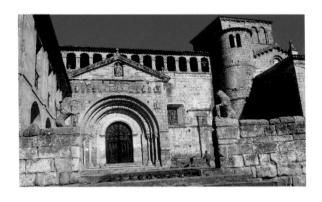

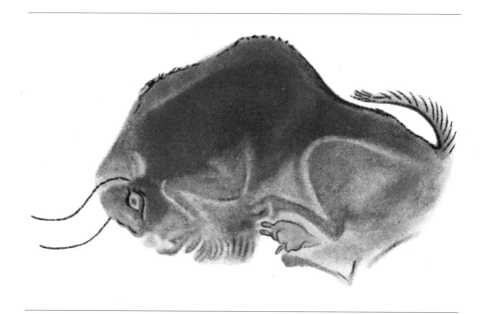